How to Enjoy Yourself After Retirement

Your Ultimate Guide to Enjoying Yourself after Retirement, Start Living a Happy, Carefree, and Financially Free

Table of Contents

Introduction

I want to thank you and congratulate you for downloading the book, *"How to Enjoy Yourself After Retirement"*.

After many years of long and hard work, you can now enjoy the fruits of your labor by going to retirement. You might be old but, you still have a number of years left in your life. Why not make the most out of your retirement? After all, you deserve to do the things you want to do after years of hard work.

This book is meant for elderly citizens who are already on their retirement years but still want to live their life to the fullest. With that, this book offers useful ideas and suggestions for retired people to consider. This book is divided into chapters:

- Chapter 1 lists the hobbies that retired people can take up during their free time.

- Chapter 2 recommends sports and outdoor activities you can engage in.

- Chapter 3 suggests life's goals that you might not have considered at first, but realize you want to accomplish before you pass on.

- Chapter 4 recommends activities for you to relax during and nurture your mind and spirit.

- Chapter 5 gives you ideas about what activities you can enjoy with your friends and loved ones.

- Chapter 6 tells you that even at such a late stage in your life, you can still get in to business ventures and tap opportunities for you to supplement your pension money.

Even with all the information in the pages of this book, you cannot truly enjoy your retirement unless you have the right attitude and mindset about facing your sunset years. Life is beautiful no matter how far you have gone and what challenges you have had to go through along the way. At this point in your life, you deserve to live happily doing the things that you truly enjoy.

Thanks again for downloading this book, I hope you enjoy it!

Chapter 1 – Taking Up Hobbies

You may already be retired from employment but that does not mean that you should simply sit back and simply watch everything around you as time ticks on. There are still a lot of things that you can do, whether on your own, with your friends, or with your family.

To start with, you can consider spending your time on a hobby. It could be a past hobby that has been set aside during your working years. Or, it could be a new hobby that you are interested to learn. With a lot of time on your hands, this is a great time to get back to your old hobby or discover a new one.

Here are a number of hobbies that you can try:

Culinary Arts

If you have skills in the kitchen, you might want to take up cooking or baking lessons. These are some of the most fun activities that you can try, because you get to enjoy the meals and desserts that you make. There are many cuisines for you to try, such as Persian, Asian, and European cuisines. The best part is that you can even impress your family and friends with the mouthwatering dishes that you make. Check out the nearest culinary schools in your area. You can also ask if your local community center or retirees group offers such classes.

Painting

Painting is one of the most popular hobbies for retirees. Aside from having a creative outlet, this hobby is known to be a good stress-reliever. Depending on your skills and interest, you can choose from a number of painting techniques or styles. You can either set up your own personal studio and paint at home or you can join art classes in your community. If budget is a consideration, you can be more creative in your choice of affordable medium of expression.

This hobby can also give you an opportunity to earn extra money by selling your paintings. Do not expect people to pay big bucks for your painting - At least, not just yet. Who know's, you might just be the next Picasso or Dali.

Writing

Writing is another stress-free activity that you can do to pass the time. There are a lot of things to write about. You have the freedom to choose what you want to write about and how you want to write it. You can choose to write fan fiction, poetry, scripts, or graphic novels among others. Anything that allows you to express yourself using the written word is perfect. Again, your writing output can also be a way for you to earn extra money. You can sell your written works or you can work as a part-time writer.

Crafts

Knitting while sitting on a rocking chair might not seem as exciting to you. But, knitting and needlecraft are not the only crafts that you can have as a hobby. Try woodworking, sculpting, or scrapbooking. There are easy crafting projects that you can start working on. As you become more skilled in your chosen craft, you can take on more complicated projects.

Studying

It is not too late to learn new things. You can choose to take up short courses at your local community college or at the nearest university if you wish. Find out if these learning institutions offer classes for senior citizens or retirees. You can also surf the net for online schools and personal tutors who can give you lessons in the field or course you are interested in.

You can go the DIY route in studying too. There are a lot of video tutorials and how-to articles online. For example, you can study graphic design by watching video tutorials on using design software such as Photoshop. You can also take up classes to learn French, Spanish, Chinese or any other foreign languages.

Dancing

Not all dance moves have to be as strenuous as all the jumping, popping, and locking of street dancing. You can go for dance genres that match your physical abilities. The waltz, the salsa, and the cha-cha are just some of the dances that are popular with the elderly. With modern technology, you do not even have to leave your home to learn the basic steps. Of course, it's more fun to take the dancing to the ballroom or dance floor whenever you can.

Photography

If you have a digital camera or a DSLR (Digital Single Lens Reflex) camera on-hand, you can pursue photography as fulfilling hobby. You can enjoy life by taking pictures of your favorite objects around the house. You can also experiment with various shots and scene modes as you take pictures of your favorite sights and subjects. You can even create a scrapbook or photo-collage and print out photos to put them in your book.

Gardening

If you have a backyard or a front lawn at home, you can take the time to plant and cultivate flowers and fruits. Gardening is great for people with a green thumb and it's a great opportunity to grow your own herb or vegetable garden for your meals. Home-grown fruits and vegetables are healthier for you and for your family. Flowers in bloom, on the other hand, are a treat for the eyes.

Blogging

If you love to write but prefer to type your thoughts online, you can take up blogging as another hobby. By blogging, you can talk about whatever issue or subject you can come up with, from guides on cooking to opinions on breaking news. You can also share your blog posts and articles to people that you know online, from friends to colleagues to former workmates.

Chapter 2 – Playing Sports and Games

Engaging in sports and active fun is the perfect way to keep your body strong and fit. There are a lot of senior citizens who continue to play sports to stay young looking and healthy. While you might think that sports activities are too strenuous, there are actually a number of sports activities that even the elderly can engage in.

Here are a number of sports that could be good for you:

Tennis and Badminton

While tennis and badminton are intense outdoor sports, they are still very enjoyable for senior citizens. These two sports are great for improving on your legwork and they are very fun to play especially when you have a partner to play with you. In addition, tennis and badminton are great to play during picnics and camping days. Just do not strain yourself by being too competitive.

Bowling

Bowling is a great recreational sport that retirees can engage in. This is a game that can be played at their own pace. They can also choose bowling balls that they can comfortably roll down the lane. Of course, this activity is not for those who have health conditions that affect vision and balance. Bowling games are also great for exercising your upper body and arms.

Basketball

Basketball is a very intense physical sport especially if it is played competitively. This does not mean that a friendly game will not give you the same health benefits. The running and jumping involved in this sport can give you a good cardiovascular exercise to keep your body and muscles in shape. Get in touch with friends so you can form teams and organize regular games.

Pro Golf

Pro golf is one of the preferred activities for retired people. It's a laid back game that does not involve a lot of movement other than the leisurely stroll on the greens. The slow pace of the game allows the retiree to take in the relaxing scenery and spend time chatting with friends. The fresh air also does wonders for your respiratory system.

Miniature Golf

If you love to play golf but cannot afford golf-course membership fees, you can also try out the miniature version. Miniature golf is just as fun and relaxing as pro-golf, plus you do not have to worry about losing golf balls in sand bunkers or ponds. In addition, mini-golf courses are also more accessible than pro-golf courses. You can bring your family and have a fun "tournament" on a weekend.

Lawn Croquet

This outdoor game involves shooting balls through metal pockets using a mallet. It is a common game played by elderly people. Lawn croquet is a nice game to play when you have friends coming over for the afternoon. The game is also perfect for exercising your mind as well as your upper body and arms. Lastly, lawn croquet is an opportunity to talk with your friends or family.

Chapter 3 – Accomplishing Life's Goals

You may have had goals and dreams during your younger years that you have not yet achieved. While hoping to achieve career goals and perhaps big dreams of becoming a billionaire might not be realistic at this time, there are some goals and dreams that could still be achievable. It's not the end of the road for you. Pick a goal or dream that you can still realistically work for. Here are some ideas:

Getting a Pet

If you live alone and you wish to get yourself a household pet, this is the perfect time to get one. Pets are your best companions around the house and they keep you occupied during your retirement. In addition, having a pet lessens your likelihood of getting depressed or lonely because they are there to keep you company.

Joining a Community Cause or Charity

If you still have the initiative to make a difference in the community, you can sign up for a charity event or cause. There are some community activities you can participate in such as feeding programs, livelihood programs, and donation drives. Contributing and helping to any cause can give you a sense of fulfillment in life which makes you feel good.

Playing Your Own Music

Music knows no age. For as long as you still have motor skills and a good ear, it is not too late to learn how to play an instrument. There are simple instruments that you can try out such as tambourines, drums, and cymbals. If you have the patience and dexterity, you can also practice harder-to-play instruments such as violin, guitar, piano, and cello. If you prefer to sing, you can take up singing lessons to improve your singing voice.

Donating to Charity

You can make a difference to society by doing charity work. You can donate your clothes, food, and other unwanted materials to those who need them. Some people might be uncomfortable giving away their stuff, but there is a rewarding feeling that comes with being able to help others. This will not only make you happy but also satisfied and content with what you have in your life.

Teaching Children

It may sometimes be considered work, but you can also enjoy life by passing on your knowledge to the next generation. If you have friends or family members who have children of their own, this is the perfect opportunity to tell stories to the kids about your experiences in the past. You can even teach them the skills you possess, such as cooking and gardening. You will surely leave a lasting mark in the minds and hearts of the children you teach.

Participating in Contests

There are various contests where you can sign up and take part. Craft-related contests such as cook-offs, bake-offs, and writing are opportunities that you can try out. There are also outdoor competitions such as fishing and golf, not to mention indoor competitions such as chess. Taking part in these contests give you a sense of thrill and adventure. Participating in the events even without winning is rewarding enough in itself. Actually winning a medal is just a bonus.

Learning How to Drive

Do this only if your reflexes and your vision are still in good condition. Instead of relying on your family to drive you around, you can learn how to drive so you can take your own leisure drives around town or to the countryside for vacation trips. Driving skills will also come in handy when you need to make emergency trips to a hospital, clinic, or police station.

Traveling

Going to places away from home might not have been possible before due to work and schedule constraints. Now, you have all the time in the world to explore and discover places that you have always wanted to visit. The great thing about travelling these days is that there are a lot of travel deals and incentives that you can find online. There are even sites and establishments that offer special discounts for retirees and senior citizens. All you have to do is to pick your destination, pack your bags, and enjoy your travel.

Finding Love

If you have never had a significant person or if you have lost a loved one in the past, maybe this is the time to seek someone you can love and be with for the rest of your life. You may find a person who interests you in places you least expect, such as the library or a public park. You may be old, but that does not mean you cannot experience love anymore.

Chapter 4 – Spending Time to Relax

After years of working hard for a living, it is now time for you to slow down and relax. Those you left behind in the rat race are still waiting for their turn to be where you are. You can now lounge around without worrying about a report that's due in a few hours or fussing over an error that could significantly delay the production line. It's time for you to stop and smell the flowers without feeling guilty about it. Consider these recommendations on activities that will help you nurture the mind and body:

Taking leisurely strolls

When you have spent most of your life working, it sometimes does not feel right for you to stay home and do nothing. Instead of relaxing you, it makes you feel more stressed. You do not have to stay cooped up. You can go for a walk around the block. You can also visit the nearest park. A leisurely stroll will give you allow you to appreciate the sights around you.

Performing muscle-relaxing exercises

Exercise is not just for getting fit and active, but also for relaxing your mind and body. There are relaxation exercises that you can take up, such as yoga and tai chi. These types of exercise can be tweaked to suit your exercise needs without straining yourself. There are classes teaching these exercises in local gyms, but you can also find exercises groups at certain times in the community park.

You can also perform relaxation exercises in the comfort of your own home. Simply find a good spot in the living room or bedroom and move furniture around to create your exercise space. To do relaxation exercises, you need to perform a series of body movements such as:

- Head stretches and twists

- Arm bends, stretches, twists, and spins

- Leg stretches and bends

- Hip twists

- Jumping jacks

Meditating

Meditation is also a great way to relax. You can do this in your own house or you can go to the nearest park or plaza. Simply find a quiet and undisturbed spot and you can begin the activity. With proper meditation, you can zone out the noise around you and focus on what is in your heart and mind. This allows you to achieve a deep state of relaxation.

Spending time in places of worship

If you are the religious type of person, you can spend quiet time in sacred buildings. There is a certain peace that can be felt when you visit places of worship. If there is a church or convent or a mosque in your area, try visiting it and stir up your spiritual side. You can even spend time with the local priest, bishop, or nun and have meaningful conversations.

Reading

You can grab yourself a novel or a pocketbook that you enjoy, find a coffee-shop, café, or other place to sit down, and read to your heart's content. If you don't have a book, a magazine or a daily newspaper will do.

Chapter 5 – Spending Quality Time with Your Family and Friends

It's time to catch up on all the quality family time you missed while you were working. You can now make the most of the time on your hands to reconnect with family and friends. There are a number of activities that you can engage in with them either in your home or in other locations.

Here are some fun and worthwhile activities that you can enjoy with your friends and family:

Board and card games

Two-player board games such as chess can keep you and your friend/partner/spouse busy, and they also keep the conversation going between you and your company. There are also multi-player games for more than two people such as Monopoly, Uno, Snakes and Ladders, and poker. These games are fun activities to have around the house, most especially during a party or group gathering.

Outdoor exercises

When the weather is fine for outdoor activities, you can head out and spend quality time with friends or family. If your area has a public park, you can take a good stroll around it or play outdoor games such as frisbee catch and badminton. If you are an energetic person in spite of your age, you can also do exercises such as jogging, running and cycling.

If your area has a nearby picnic area or camping site, you can spend a day with friends or family by having an outdoor picnic. If the site has outdoor games and competitions, feel free to take part in those games, as long as you go have fun with other people. If outdoor community activities do not suit you, you can have a peaceful hiking activity with your friends along the hills or other places in your area.

Housekeeping and other errands

Household errands need not to be boring as long as everyone helps out and keeps each other company. If you have other family members living with you at home, you can take the time to help them with chores around the house. You can help your spouse, children, or grandchildren with some tasks such as cleaning, cooking, and gardening. While you help them around the house, you can ask questions and tell stories to keep them entertained.

Libraries and other community or commercial areas

If you are very interested in reading, you can pay a visit to a nearby public library where you can spend time reading books and other materials along with your friends. The library is also is a great place to enjoy tranquility even without company, as there are thousands of books, magazines, and newspapers to keep you entertained. Best of all, you can borrow books for reading outside the premises and these books can keep you busy at home.

Community events

You can also check your area for main attractions or events that you can go to. Such events like concerts, seminars, conventions, expos and fairs are a welcome alternative for you and your friends/relatives to spend time together. It is even more welcoming if the events are much more participative such as workshops.

Chapter 6 – Trying Out Business Ventures

There are times when your pension might not be enough to cover your expenses. Even when it is, surely, you would not let a good opportunity to earn more income pass. Old age should not stop you from becoming an entrepreneur if you want to. You simply have to choose the kind of business that matches your skills and will not be too taxing for you to manage.

You can try out these business ventures:

Vending-machine operation

One of the most reliable small businesses to earn money is through the vending-machine business. The great thing about this is that they don't require too much activity or labor on your part. You can set up these machines in places such as tourist landmarks, offices, schools, malls, and recreational parks. You can even set them up in your retirement home if you want to capitalize on the place. It will require weekly visits to replenish stock and inspect for needed repairs and maintenance, but that's a small price to pay for a thriving business.

Multi-level marketing

In spite of controversies, this option is actually a good way to earn money without having to do too much work. These opportunities offer a variety of products that you have to sell, and it takes a lot of networking in order to sell them to different people. Fortunately, some companies offer training seminars and workshops in order to get you more capable and motivated to sell these products. Choose your MLM company wisely and stay away from scams.

Real-estate / Rental property

If you have an extra piece of property that you acquired in the past, you can make money out of it by putting it up for rent. Rental income can help you in case your monthly pension is not enough, plus the sideline does not take up too much time. On the other hand, you can try out real-estate by selling property to other people and earn commissions for each sold house. Any of the two sidelines can benefit you as they both provide good income.

Selling items online

If you have a lot of antiques and collected items that you do not use anymore, you can simply sell them in online sites such as eBay and Craiglist. You can also sell any art or craft that you made during your spare time, such as paintings, wooly blankets, wood decorations, and manuscripts. Online selling is a great way to make money while still enjoying the free time.

Catering sideline

You can take advantage of your cooking and baking skills by putting up a food business. Catering is a great way to earn additional money while doing something that you like. Come up with your signature dishes and desserts to differentiate you from other caterers in your area.

Selling paperback or digital books

If you have written pocketbooks or stories and you want to release them for sale, you can sell your written material in an online market such as Amazon or eBay. Published books can bring you money, which is a great way to earn additional income.

Offer your services

If you are a professional, you can still use your skills to offer your services to private clients. It could be a consultancy of sorts or maybe even gigs for teaching small groups of people particular skills. Accountants, programmers, and financial analysts are some of those whose services are normally sought after. Those from the medical field can also offer to take on transcription projects or teach first aid at the local community center.

Conclusion
Do not fill out I will fill out Conclusion myself

Thank you again for downloading this book!

I hope this book was able to help you to enjoy your life after retirement. In spite of your age, you can still do a lot of things in life, and these things can make you feel happier and livelier even in your retirement. Likewise, you also make other people happy as you do some things such as playing games and taking part in community events. Taking part in those things also make you happy because you see other people becoming so happy.

The next step is to keep bringing joy and happiness as you keep doing the things you love and keep other people company. In addition, as you reach the final years of your life, your next step is to pass on your knowledge and skills to other people such as your grandchildren, your children, and even your friends. With the years that you have left, you can hopefully train them to learn the same ways you have learned in the past.

Finally, if you enjoyed this book, then I'd like to ask you for a favor, would you be kind enough to leave a review for this book on Amazon? It'd be greatly appreciated!

Click here to leave a review for this book on Amazon!

Thank you and good luck!

www.ingramcontent.com/pod-product-compliance
Lightning Source LLC
Chambersburg PA
CBHW070527210526
45168CB00022B/1739